JAZZ GUITAR TECHNIQUE

ANDREW GREEN

Jazz Guitar Technique

Andrew Green

Microphonic Press
500 2nd St. #3
Brooklyn, NY 11215

www.microphonicpress.com

Cover Design: Andrew Green
Interior Design: Emerson Nyswans

ISBN 0-9700576-1-X

Thanks to:

John McNeil
Lolly Bienenfeld
Willie Smith
Sarth Calhoun
Bill DeArango
Bonnie Ralston
Bob Montgomery

Visit the Jazz Guitar Technique Web site at:

www.chopsfactory.com

CONTENTS

INTRODUCTION

When improvising, what your mind hears is more often than not determined by what your body can reproduce on your instrument. Much of your conception as an improviser is determined by your technique. If you can't play certain types of ideas, you are simply not going to conceive of them while you are improvising. Even if you could, it wouldn't matter, since you couldn't play them anyway.

There are many melodic structures that are physically challenging to play on the guitar. For example, anything that necessitates playing consecutive notes on adjacent strings presents logistical problems for both hands. This includes various arpeggios, triad-based lines, consecutive fourths, and large interval leaps. Since these melodic devices present such a challenge, the range of ideas in a typical guitar solo doesn't include them.

To expand the palette of musical ideas available to you as an improviser, you must expand your technique. The way to do this is to practice things that feature physically challenging motion. By playing lines that incorporate new and different types of melodic movement, you gain the technical ability necessary to improvise with these structures, and the sound of these melodies will gradually enter your musical consciousness.

The exercises in this book will improve your technique, increase the range of your ideas, and open up new avenues of improvisation to you. You, in turn will have the opportunity to add to the vocabulary of what is possible to play on the guitar.

HOW TO USE THIS BOOK

BASICS I — LEARNING THE NECK
If you are not sure of where all of the notes are on the neck of the guitar, start here.

BASICS II — PICKING
Exercises to develop assurance with your right hand.

CROSS-STRING STUDIES
Picking across two strings, three strings, and finally, four. Each group starts with exercises and continues with musical examples and lines that can be used as etudes.

TRIADS
Major and Minor triad arpeggios across all six strings. These are great warm-ups.

COMPLEX RHYTHMS
Rhythms, first on one note, then applied to melodic lines.

ADVANCED STUDIES
A line compendium featuring exercises and examples that incorporate ideas from all of the previous sections.

PHRASING
Exercises that will help shape the ideas generated by your increasing technical skill.

GRABBING CHORDS
Exercises designed to enable you to play chord voicings without hesitation.

LINES AND CHORDS
Eighth note lines mixed with chord voicings.

ETUDES
10 page-length studies that feature all of the single note ideas in this book.

SUGGESTIONS FOR PRACTICE

1. **Always use a metronome.** Practicing at a consistent tempo allows your body and mind to coordinate more easily. You can also avoid the common pitfalls of speeding up when playing something easy and slowing down when playing something difficult. If you are reading something for the first time, set the metronome at a tempo that is slow enough so that you can play without stopping. It doesn't matter how slow that turns out to be.

2. **Warm up slowly.** A slow warm-up helps your hands get accustomed to the work they have to do. Guitarists are athletes from the elbow out to the fingers, and since athletes warm up and stretch out before they play, so should you. Start playing scales or arpeggios slowly, with a metronome. Choose things that are familiar and are easy to execute. I recommend doing this for the first fifteen minutes at least.

3. **Practice a small number of things until you own them.** In addition to the warm-up (scales or arpeggios) pick two things to practice. You could choose a line from **Advanced Studies** (page 66) and some exercises from **Lines and Chords** (page 94). Whatever you choose, play those things and *only* those things. If you practice too many different things, you tend to water down the learning process.

4. **Take a break every once in a while so you don't hurt yourself.** This is especially important when playing things that stretch the boundaries of your technique. It is far better to play for twenty minutes at a time and then take a break, than to play for four hours and risk tendinitis.

5. **Play the examples in this book in different keys and different areas of the guitar neck.** Many of the exercises will feel very different when played in other keys or octaves (see page 75).

6. **Apply different rhythms.** The music in this book is predominantly written as eighth note lines to emphasize the technical challenges involved. Applying different rhythms to the exercises and examples (see page 58) enables you to derive the greatest benefit from the material.

A QUICK DISCUSSION OF FINGERING

Most of the time in this book, I will not talk about specific fingerings for the left hand. Generally, when playing phrases that involve notes on adjacent strings at the same fret, use the longer finger to fret the lower string. For example:

This fingering may seem odd at first, but it makes difficult passages easier in the long run. There is more discussion of this fingering method in **Triads**, beginning on page 52.

String and Finger Indications

Strings are indicated with circled numbers below the staff; ⑥ is the low E string, ① is the high E string.

Left hand fingerings are shown as:

1 = index finger
2 = middle finger
3 = ring finger
4 = little finger

BASICS I — LEARNING THE NECK

To improvise freely on the guitar, you need to be able to play the same idea in many different places on the neck. Otherwise, you could find yourself playing at the twelfth fret, hear an idea that you only know how to play at the fifth fret and not be able to execute it.

First, you must know where all of the notes are at all times. Then you need to learn every possible location for everything you play – scales, chords, arpeggios, you name it.

While you will undoubtedly develop your own favorite ways to play things, knowing all of the possibilities allows you to make *choices*.

Beginning guitar technique usually involves learning scales and arpeggios "in position." Improvising freely, on the other hand, necessitates being able to move quickly from position to position, in effect eliminating the concept of playing "in position" altogether.

Here are some exercises to develop familiarity with the neck. Follow the string and finger indications to get the intended benefit.

1

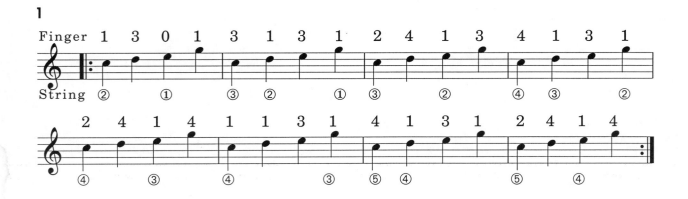

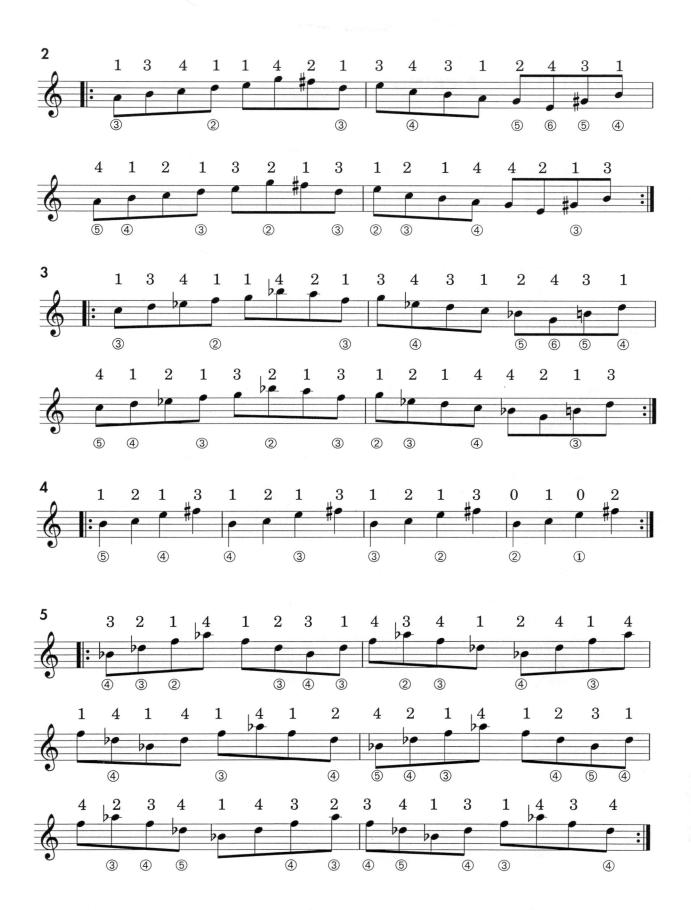

BASICS II — PICKING

Your picking hand needs to produce the desired volume and emphasis for each note you play. Having this control not only gives your playing confidence and authority, but helps develop good time. To gain this control, there are several things you need to do:

Practice with a metronome. Always use a metronome when you practice. A metronome tells you one thing only: how fast you're going. It doesn't help you swing or be more creative, it just plays the pulse. Practicing with a metronome reinforces the idea of playing everything in time.

You can emulate a drummer's hi-hat by placing the metronome on beats two and four. If you want to play with a backbeat, put the metronome on beat three. If you are reading something for the first time, set the metronome at a tempo that is slow enough so that you can play without mistakes.

Play simple rhythmic ideas. Playing a simple rhythmic phrase with the metronome will help give your playing a solid feel and develop assertiveness with your picking hand. To practice this technique:

Hear the metronome on all four beats (at first).

Play the phrases on page 13 in order, starting with #1.

Play each phrase for 5 or 10 minutes at a stretch, or until it "locks in" and really feels solid.

Do this on a daily basis, and over a short span of time you will start to notice that your picking hand has developed more authority.

CROSS-STRING STUDIES

Picking across the strings (one note per string) is more difficult than playing several notes on each string. The exercises in this section address this aspect of guitar technique.

Start with the two-string interval studies. These may seem easy at first, but playing them at fast tempos will make the technical challenge apparent. The interval studies start with one note per string, then three-note groups with two notes on the lower string, one on the upper string; then two notes on the upper string, one on the lower; and finally four-note groups with two notes on each string.

The three-string studies feature triad fragments and other structures commonly heard in modern jazz. Like the two-string studies, these also introduce two notes on successive strings. There is more variation in the three-string exercises since the range of possibilities is greater.

The last group of exercises is based on arpeggios across three and four strings. I find that playing across four strings is one of the more challenging things to do on the guitar. This skill is also one of the first things to disappear if I don't practice it for a while.

Following each group of exercises are phrases and examples that utilize the string combinations and techniques developed in the exercises.

Follow the string and finger indications. After playing the exercises in the original locations on the neck, try them in different keys and string combinations.

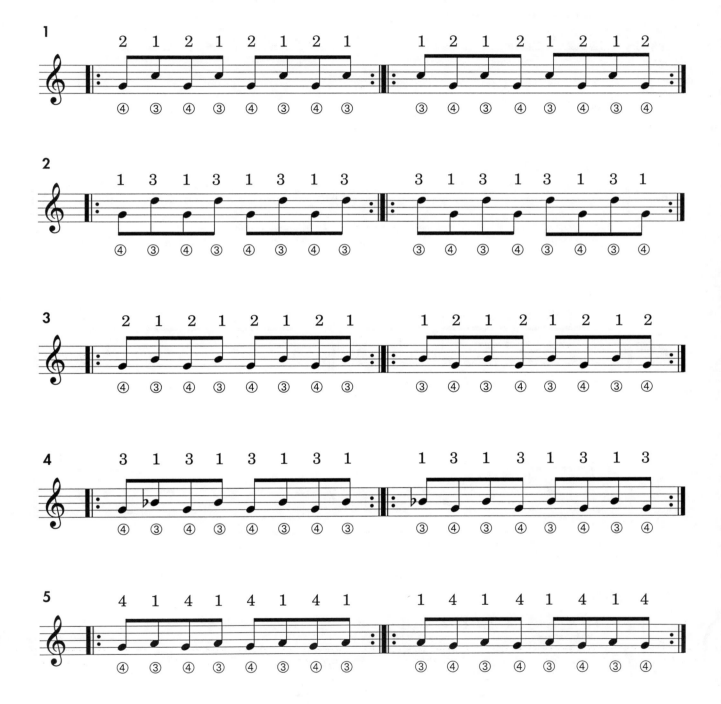

TWO-STRING EXERCISES: Two Notes on the Lower String

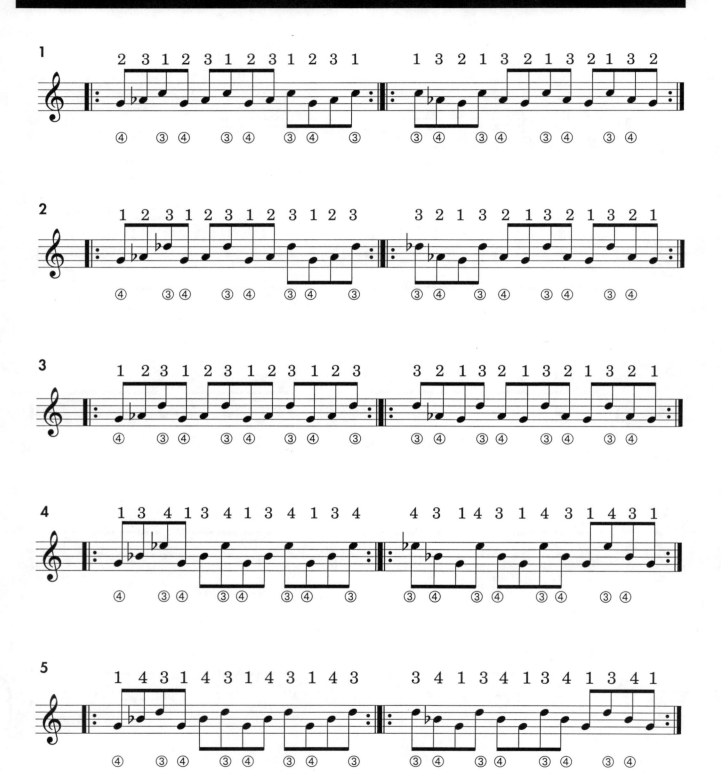

6

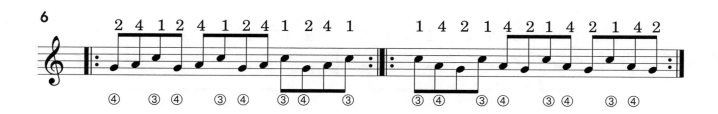

7

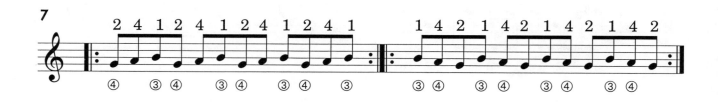

8

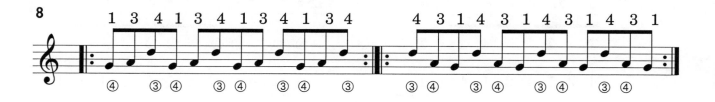

9

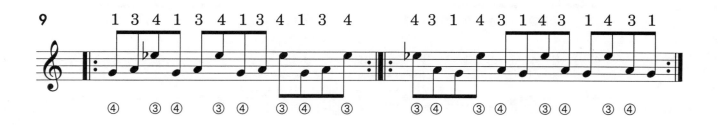

10

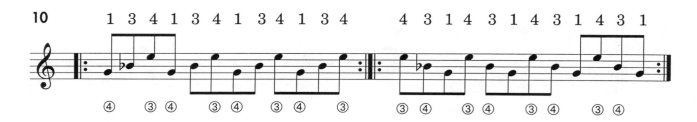

MORE ➡

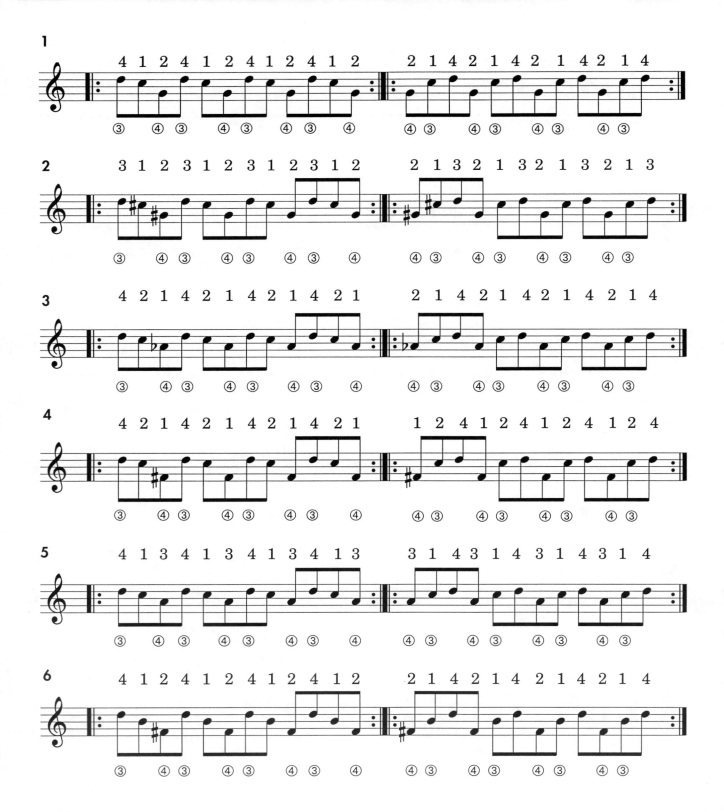

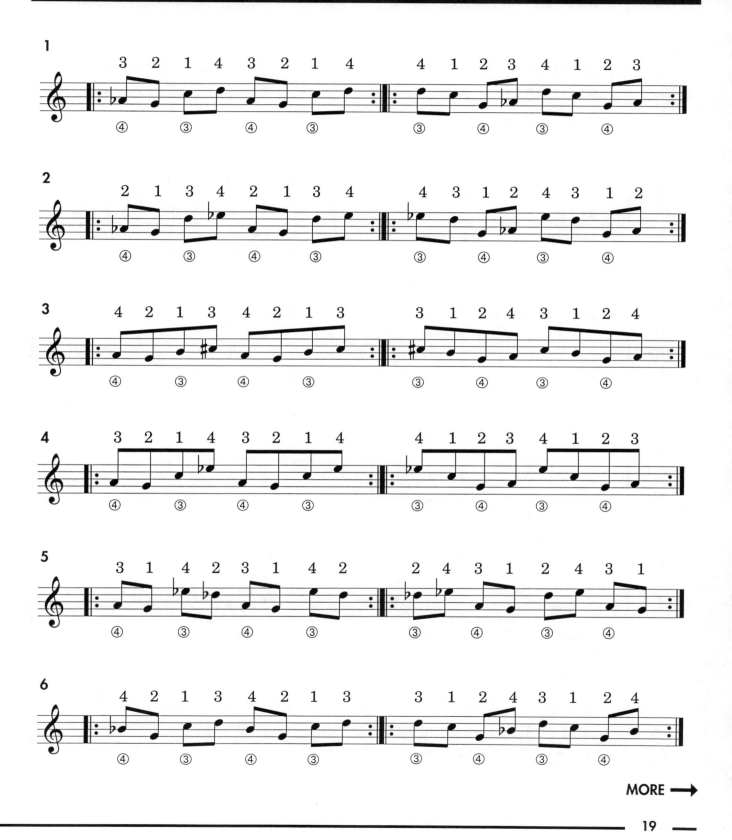

MORE ➡

TWO-STRING EXERCISES: Two Notes on Each String

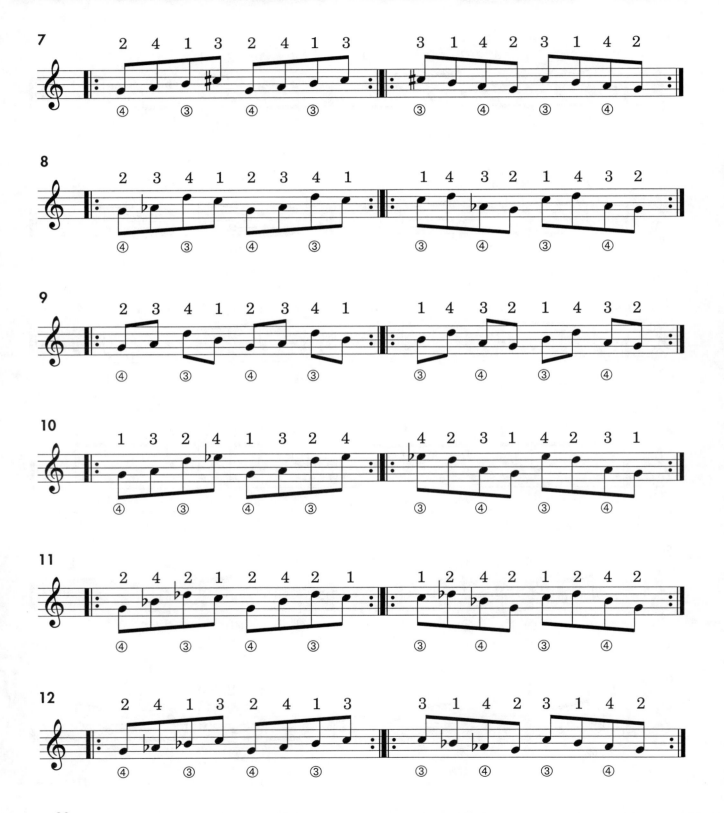

1

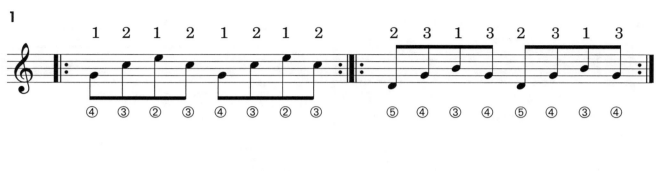

2

3

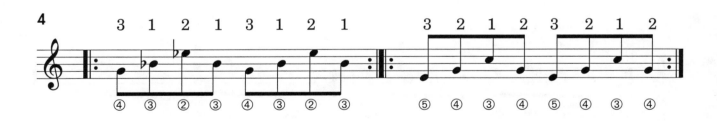

4

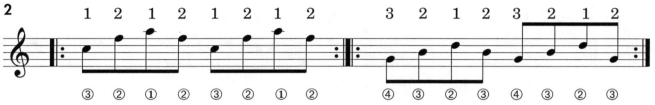

5

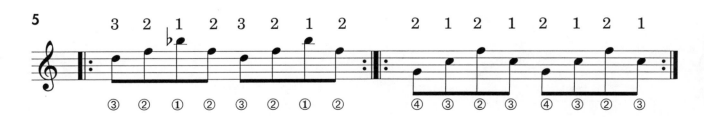

MORE ➡

THREE-STRING EXERCISES

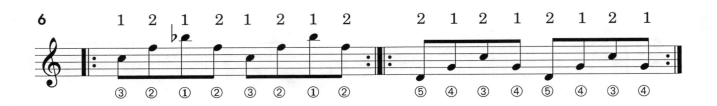

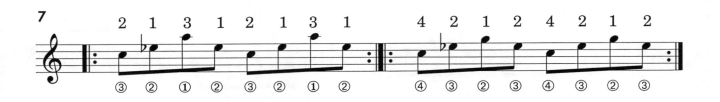

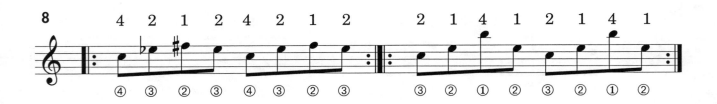

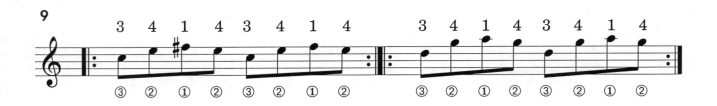

1

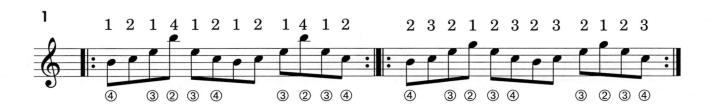

2

3

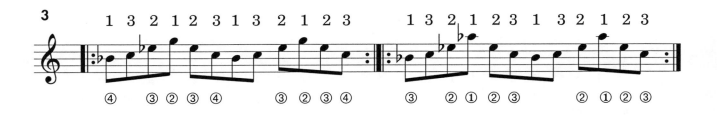

4

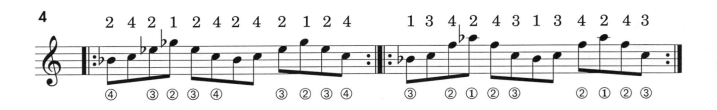

5

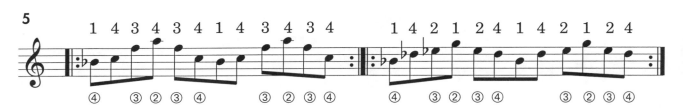

MORE →

1

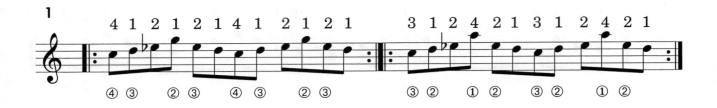

2

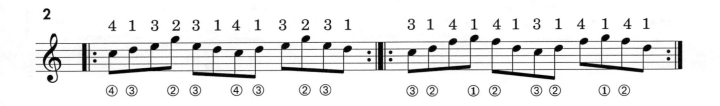

3

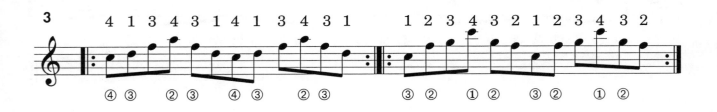

4

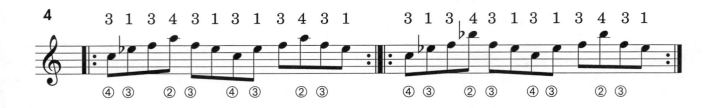

5

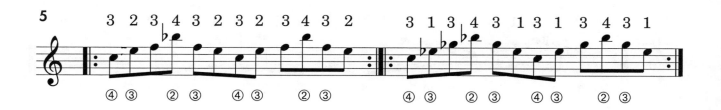

6

7

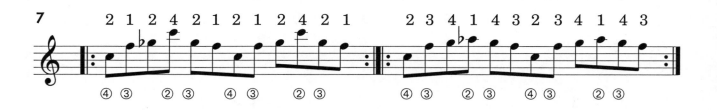

8

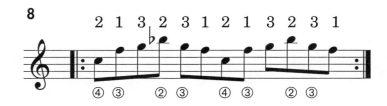

MORE ➡

THREE-STRING EXERCISES: Two Notes on the Highest String

1

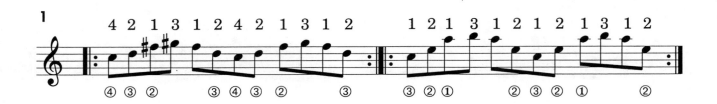

2

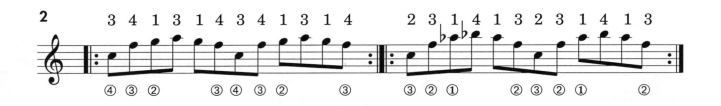

3

4

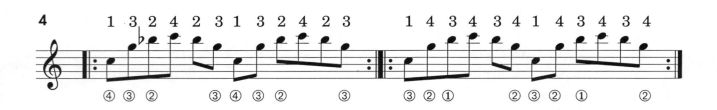

5

1

2

3

4

5

MORE ➡

6

7

8

9

10

MORE →

MORE →

25

26

27

28

29

30

31

32

33

34

MORE ➡

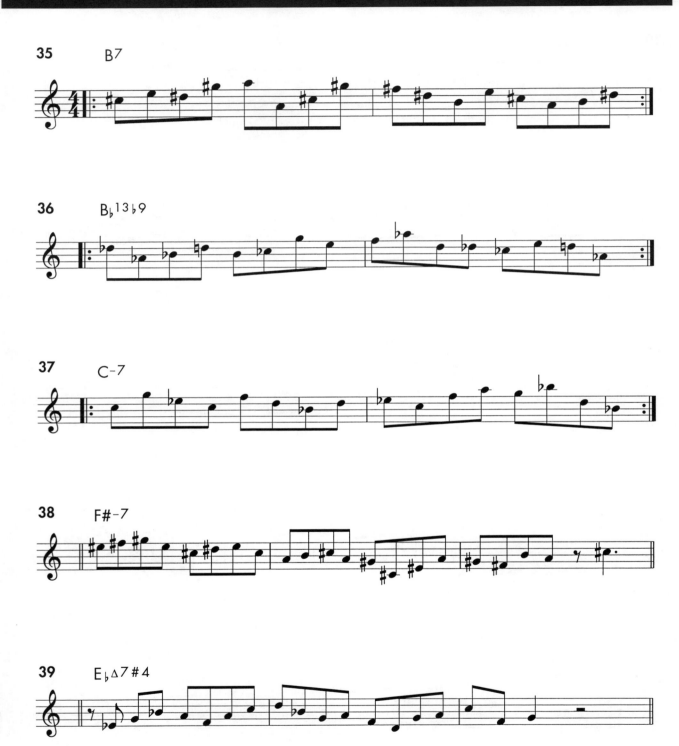

40 E–7 phryg.

41 E♭7#4

42 A–7 phryg.

43 E–7

44 C7

MORE →

45   GΔ7#4

46   DbΔ7#4

47   F-7phryg.

48   C-

49   Bb7

50 D-7phryg.

51

52

53

54

THREE AND FOUR-STRING ARPEGGIOS

1

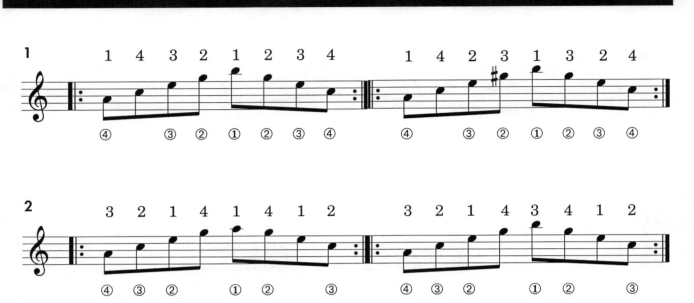

2

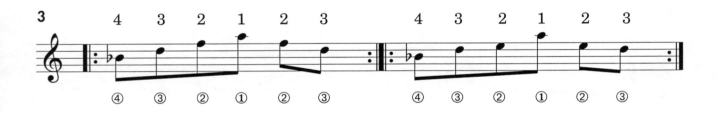

3

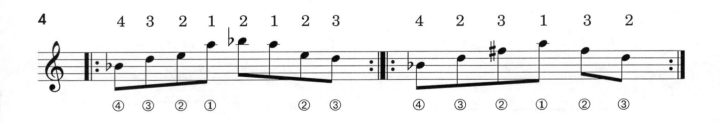

4

5

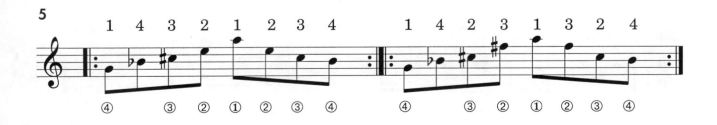

6

7

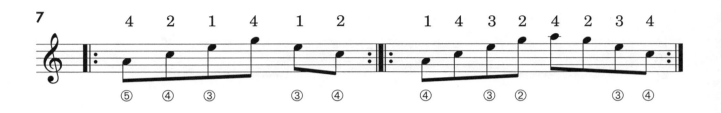

8

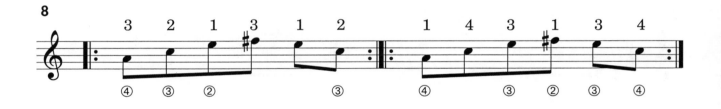

9

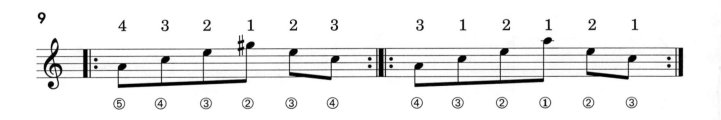

10

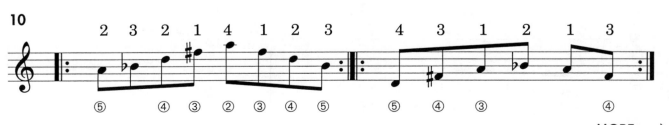

MORE ➡

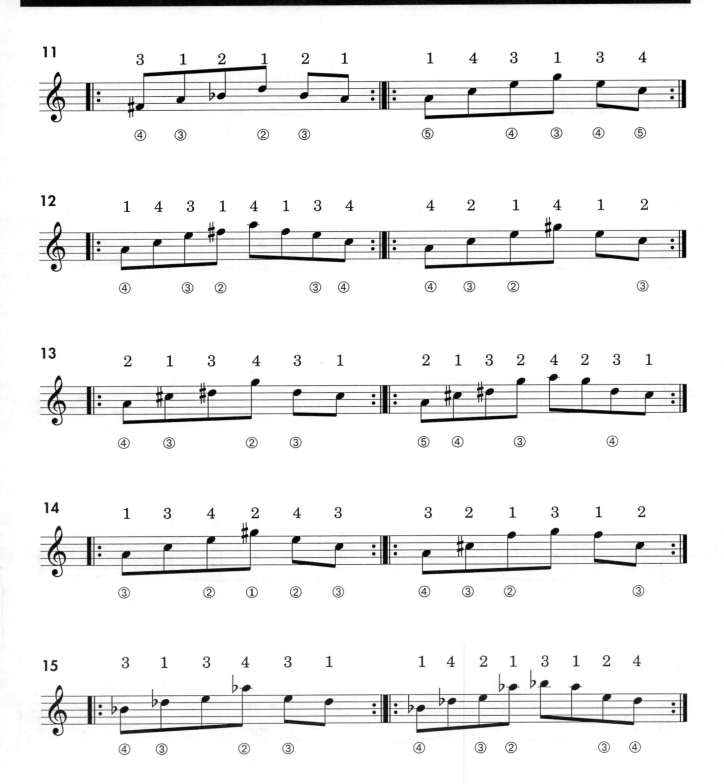

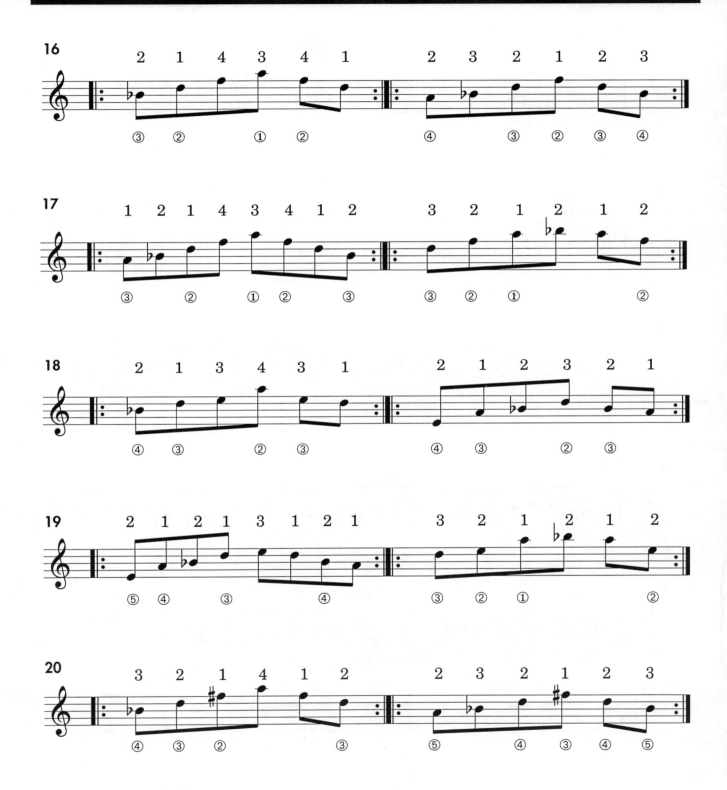

MORE ➡

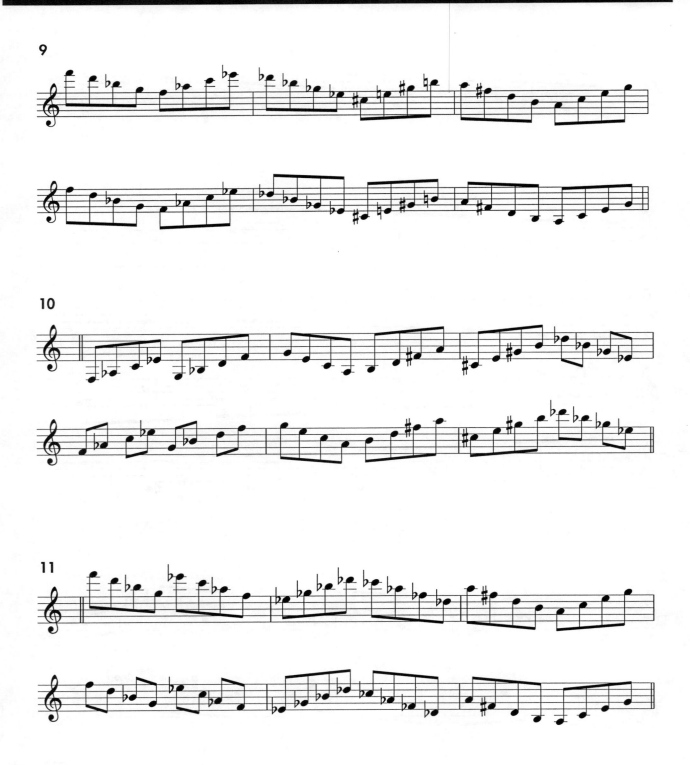

12

13

14

15

16

MORE ➡

17

18

19

20

21

22

23

24

25

26

MORE ➡

32 C7

33 E♭–7

34 G–7phryg.

35 F#–7

36 F–7

MORE →

37   B7+4

38   C△7+4

39   C−7

40   Bb△7+4

41   Ab7+4

42 Db7+4

43 Bb-7

44 C-7   Dø   G7alt

45 Cø   F7alt   Bb-7

46 C7b9

TRIADS

Using arpeggiated triads is an excellent way to bring coherence to an improvised solo. They are easy for the listener to hear and for the improviser to conceive. Triads are useful for playing motivic ideas and implying different harmonies over chord changes.

On guitar, improvising with triads presents a technical challenge because it involves playing consecutive notes on adjacent strings, often at the same fret. To meet the challenge, you must develop effective habits for fingering and picking.

On pages 54-57 are five different fingering positions for two-octave arpeggios across six strings, as well as three positions for playing up and down the neck, all in the key of G. Because the fingerings shown do not involve any open strings, they can be used in every key.

The basic rationale for these fingerings is that when given a choice of fingers with which to play consecutive notes on adjacent strings at the same fret, the longer finger should play on the lower string (see the example on page 9). An exception would be when you have *three* consecutive notes on adjacent strings at the same fret. In this case, choose a fingering that allows you to end up in the most logical position, i.e., the one that enables further movement up the highest of the three strings. See the fourth position on page 54 for an example.

My suggested fingerings are not mandatory. One thing I will emphasize: Don't barre when playing consecutive notes at the same fret — this makes it harder to play with good time and, more importantly, can contribute to tendinitis.

Arpeggiated triads are also a challenge for the right hand. Picking across consecutive strings requires a lot of control, which only comes from consistent practice.

To pick across strings, you have several options:

1) Strict alternate picking; 2) Sweep picking, in which all of the notes moving in one direction are picked in that direction; 3) A combination of the above (alternate pick going up, sweep pick going down, or vice versa).

Choose the one that feels the most comfortable for you.

Practicing triads will not only strengthen your left and right hand technique, it will change the way you organize your musical ideas relative to the guitar and open up more possibilities for playing other structures and ideas.

Practicing Triads

Practice triads in each position and in every key. Use a metronome set at half note = 60, playing the triads as quarter notes. This slow tempo allows you to develop *control*, the crucial element in good technique.

Strive to play each note at the same volume and make sure that it rings until the next note is played (legato).

Start each key with the lowest possible fingering position. Play each position four times.

When you first start to practice triad arpeggios, take a break after every three or four keys. It is especially important to do this when playing anything that is new or different physically.

Advanced Practice

When you have gotten comfortable playing triads in all positions in all keys (meaning you can play them legato, at an even volume and remain relaxed while doing so), practice them using progressive rhythmic subdivision.

Keeping the same slow tempo, play the first position as quarter notes two times; then as quarter note triplets two times; eighth notes two times; eighth note triplets two times; and finally sixteenth notes two times. Then, move to the next position and repeat the process, etc.

Most likely, the eighth note triplets and sixteenth notes won't come out cleanly at first. This is to be expected. **Repeating the motion, without worrying about the results, is what allows the desired result to happen.**

This practice technique is less taxing on your hands because you're not making constant demands on them to play at the extreme limit of their ability. Even so, when you first start to do this exercise, you might want to limit the subdivision to eighth notes. Add the eighth note triplets and the sixteenth notes later.

This method of tempo subdivision makes it easier to coordinate your hands and mind because you have a consistent pulse to work with. Subdividing one tempo (so that it is exactly twice as fast), as opposed to playing at a faster, but different, tempo is also less taxing mentally. You can apply this method to whatever you practice.

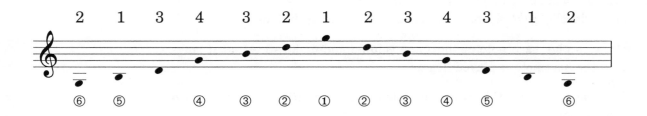

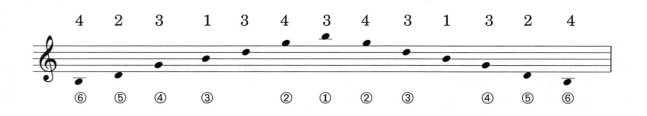

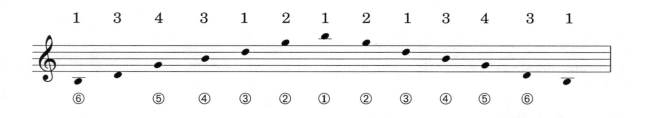

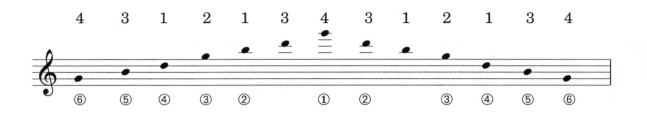

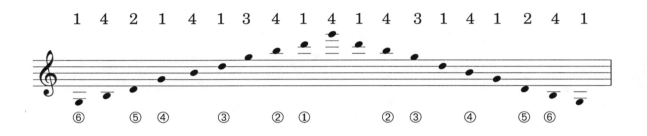

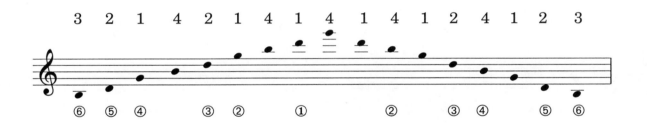

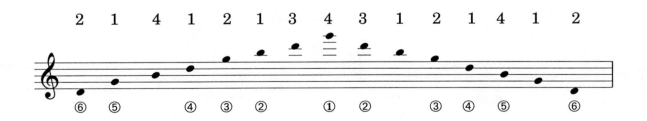

MORE ➡

MINOR TRIADS: Across Six Strings

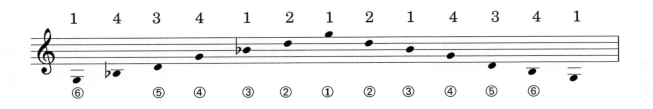

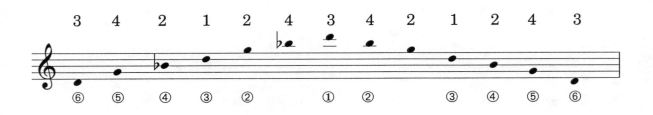

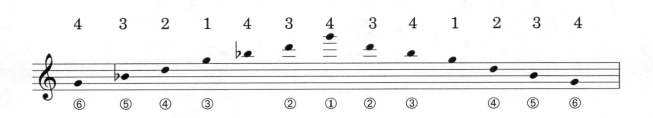

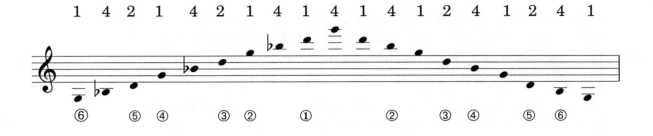

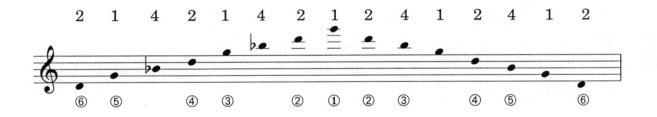

COMPLEX RHYTHMS

A way to gain further skill with the picking hand is to play increasingly complex rhythmic ideas. This presents a different challenge than playing long eighth-note lines. In addition, practicing these rhythms improves your reading.

The ability to play rhythmic ideas is a valuable skill for an improviser to have, especially when it comes to motivic development in a solo (as opposed to running eighth-note lines). Depending on the style and the feel/tempo of the tune, you might play up to 70% motivic and 30% eighth-note lines.

The following exercises are intended to get progressively more challenging. Each one appears first as a basic rhythm, then as a melodic line. The melodic lines represent one possibility. You can and should apply your own melodies to the rhythms.

Metronome markings are given for an upper limit practice tempo. To start with, play the exercises at a tempo that is slow enough so that you can play without stopping.

1

2

3

4

5

MORE ➞

6

7

8

9

10

11

12

13

14

15

MORE ➔

16

17

18

19

20

21

22

23

24

25

MORE →

26

27a

27b

28a

28b

ADVANCED STUDIES

Having "chops" is not just having the ability to play fast — it is having the freedom to play what you want. If you can only play scales at any tempo, you don't necessarily have chops. Listening to someone running scales in a solo is about the most boring thing I can think of. Playing ideas with interesting contours, rhythms and harmonies is what really counts.

To be able to make musical choices regardless of tempo, requires a great deal of technical skill. The more choices you can make, the more freedom you have and the more you can express yourself.

This section of the book consists of ten pages of lines that seek to broaden the technical boundaries of the guitar. The studies combine elements of the previous chapters and are drawn from the modern jazz idiom. Each example presents specific fingering or picking challenges, or both.

The studies incorporate a diverse range of harmonic and linear ideas. Many incorporate familiar arpeggios and scales, while others are made up of triads, interval-based lines or combinations of the above. They feature motion that is, to my knowledge, not commonly used in the language of the guitar, as of the early 21st century.

Most of the studies are written over chord changes. You could play any of these lines in a solo, but you'll probably want to use them as examples in creating your own.

1   F7

2   G7

3   F7

4   G−7   C7   FΔ7

(A♭−7   D♭7)

5   G−7   C7   FΔ7

MORE ➡

6

7

8

9

10

11

12

13

14

15

MORE →

MORE ➜

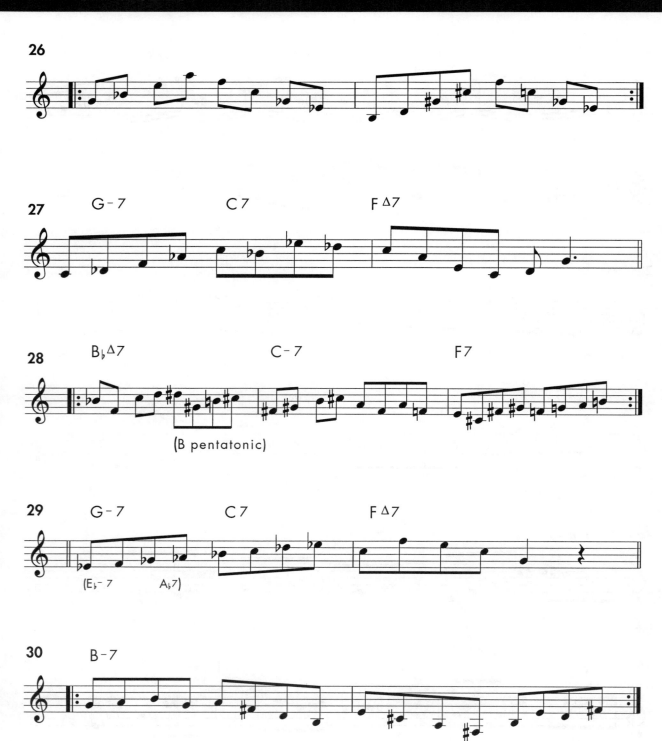

31

32

33

34

35

MORE ➡

36   C–7

37   B♭7

38   B♭△7   G7   C–7   F7

39   F7

40   C7#4♭9   F–7

PHRASING

Picking/Slurring/Hammering/Accenting

One way to increase the interest within an eighth-note line is by varying attack and volume. This is done to achieve a more vocal quality in your playing. A quick perusal (better yet, a long perusal), of any Charlie Parker solo, for example, will give you an idea of the rise and fall of attack and volume that happens within a well-conceived line. You will quickly realize that Bird's phrases don't consist of a stream of endless eighth notes played with no articulation.

Horn players and vocalists shape their phrases and dynamics through control of their air stream and through tonguing or articulation. There are several ways in which guitarists can emulate these aspects of phrasing:

Slurring ("S")/Hammering ("H") — After first picking a note, playing a higher note by fretting it without picking again.

Sliding ("Sl") — Playing a note one fret below the desired note and moving up to it using the same finger. This happens faster than a slur or hammer, so that the effect is of one attack not two.

Pull off ("P") — Picking the first note then playing a lower note by pulling the string with the finger that fretted the first note.

Accenting (">") — Picking some notes harder, therefore louder, than others.

The general idea is to pick on the upbeats and either hammer/slur or pull off on the downbeats. The notes that aren't picked will be slightly softer, allowing for variation from note to note within a line. Add to this the concept of varying the accents on the notes you *do* pick, and you have gone a long way toward achieving a more swinging, less monotonous sound.

Try playing the following:

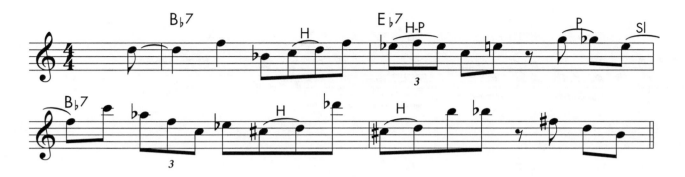

Notice that within the phrase, not only were some notes louder than others, but it had a more vocal quality overall.

Some kinds of melodic movement lend themselves to this technique more than others. A heavily arpeggiated line, for instance, does not have as many places where slurring/hammering can take place, since you're playing only one note per string. If you use the phrasing where possible however, you will still achieve the desired effect:

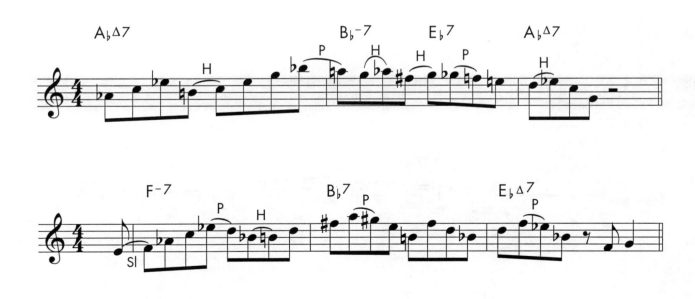

Playing unevenly accented note groupings within a line of eighth notes is another way to increase the swing quotient. Compare the following lines:

Notice that the line with even accents sounds predictable, while the line with displaced accents is more interesting. The line with displaced accents is trickier to play, but anything that you can do to make your playing more exciting is worth pursuing.

Accenting within a line requires right hand control. To gain this facility, practice the following exercises featuring random accents within different types of melodic structures.

ACCENTING EXERCISES

Another way to increase interest is to vary the harmonic rhythm in your improvised phrases. If every phrase lines up exactly with every chord, it quickly becomes boring.

To create more interest:

Alter the duration of some chord changes. If you are improvising on chords that last one bar apiece, for example, treat some measures as if they were five beats long and some as if they were three beats long:

Anticipate some chords. Playing melodies that fit the chord change following the one that is currently being played produces more forward motion:

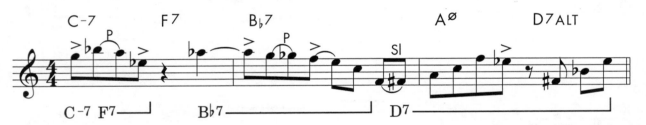

Delay resolutions to some chords. Extend a dominant chord sound into the measure in which it would normally resolve:

A study of any of the great Jazz improvisers will reveal just how often these techniques are used in any well conceived solo.

To get extra use out of the following exercises:

- Play the exercises with the accent and slur indications
- Play them by picking every note to get right hand practice

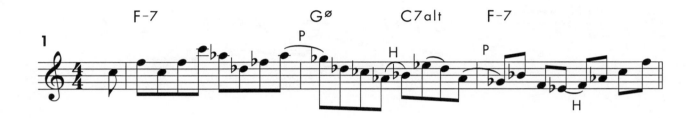

MORE ➡

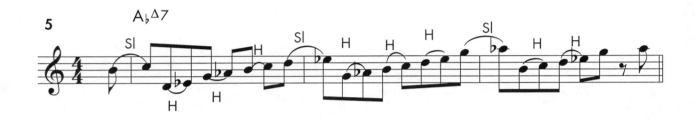

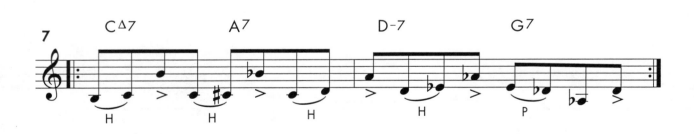

9

10

11

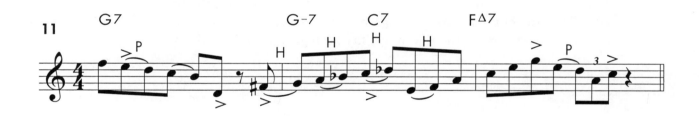

12

GRABBING CHORDS

Being able to grab chord voicings easily is vital for comping behind melodies and solos, and for filling out your own solos if you are the only chord instrument present. Grabbing voicings presents a challenge for your left hand because you often have to change the position of all four fingers simultaneously.

The following exercises should be practiced with specific rhythms and with a metronome. Even if you don't play one of the voicings cleanly, keep going; don't lose the time no matter what. If you allow yourself extra time to grab a voicing, you won't get the benefit of the practice.

A further challenge regarding chord grabbing is playing the voicings with **no space in between**. In addition to producing a very distinctive effect, it provides great left hand practice.

The first exercises use a D Dorian Mode (C Major scale from D to D) voiced in fourths. The voicings can be played on either the middle four strings or the top four. Play both groups of fingerings up *and* down.

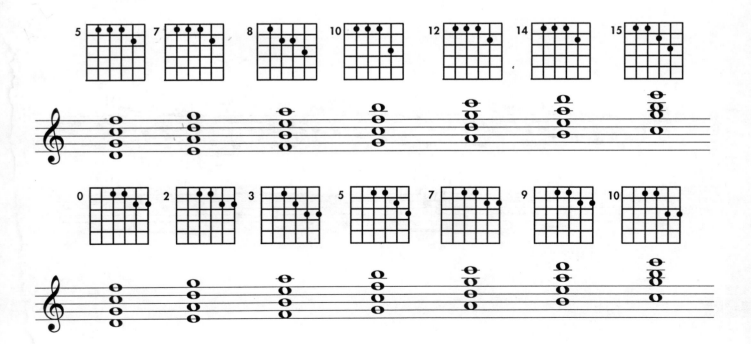

Voicings in fourths can be used for several different chord qualities:

D-7

G13

F△7+4

E-7phryg.

Voicings in fourths over II-7 V7 I progressions in major and minor:

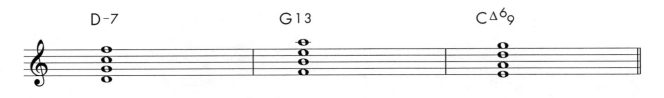

These voicings can be changed by one note to create other chord types and to create altered dominants when needed. This also varies the fingering patterns involved.

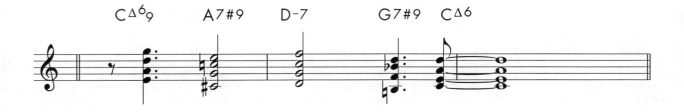

The next group of exercises uses the Diminished Scale harmonized with two voicings which form a repeating pattern. The second voicing is a very familiar one for $C^{7\#9}$.

$C^{7\flat9/\#9}$ harmonized with the Diminished Scale using two chord voicings:

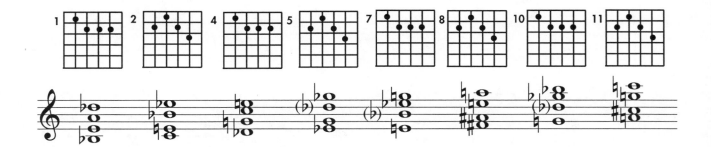

Here's how it looks on the top four strings (starting from the lowest available note):

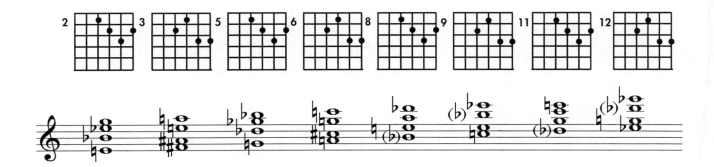

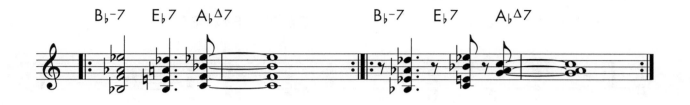

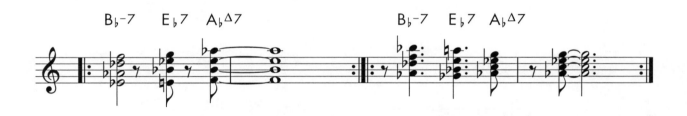

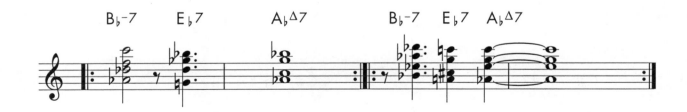

MORE →

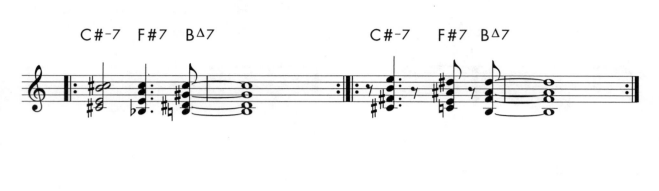

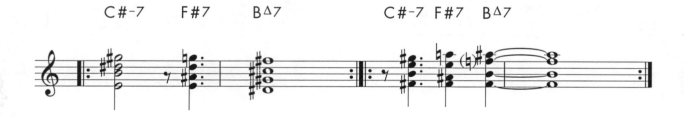

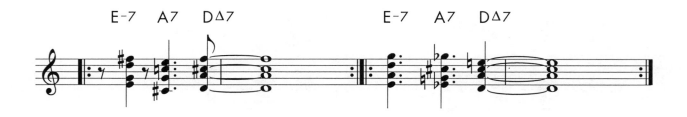

MORE ➡

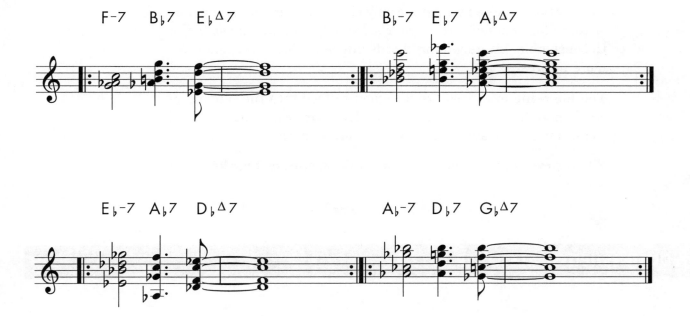

LINES and CHORDS

In situations where you are the only chord instrument, being able to comp for yourself during your solos helps fill out the sound of the ensemble. Interspersing chords into your lines also generates more interest.

The following exercises are designed to facilitate the playing of single note lines mixed with chords. This improves your left hand coordination in ways that no other exercise does.

When practicing these exercises, take frequent breaks.

DIMINISHED SCALE OVER B♭13♭9

F–7   B♭7 (throughout)

MORE ➡

BLUES IN C

MORE →

MORE ➡

MORE →

MORE ➡

APPENDIX

90 Reasons Why You Need Good Technique

Afro-Centric
Ah-Leu-Cha
Airegin
All God's Chillun' Got Rhythm
Baghdad Blues
Bebop
Beyond All Limits
Birdlike
Blowin' the Blues Away
Blues Connotation
Blues on the Corner
Break City
Brilliant Corners
B. Quick
B. Swift
Calcutta Cutie
Caravan
Cherokee
Confirmation
Cookin' at the Continental
Countdown
Daahoud
Dance of the Infidels
Donna Lee
Dr. Jackle
ESP
Eternal Triangle
Evidence
Eye of the Hurricane
Four By Five
Freedom Jazz Dance
Gazelle
Giant Steps
Gingerbread Boy
Grand Central
Hot House
Hub-Tones

Impressions
In n' Out
Inner Urge
Isotope
Jinrikisha
Joshua
Joy Spring
Just One of Those Things
Litha
Locomotion
May-Reh
Miles' Mode
Milestones
Mr. P.C.
Mode For Joe
Mohawk
Moment's Notice
Moontrane
Moose the Mooche
Move
My Shining Hour
Oscar for Treadwell
One Finger Snap
Parisian Thoroughfare
Passion Dance
Passport
Pent-Up House
Punjab
Pursuance
Quasimodo
Quicksilver
Room 608
Sandu
Satellite
Secret Love
Seven Steps to Heaven
Shaw 'Nuff

Sidecar
Sippin' at Belle's
Sorcerer
Taurus People
The Bridge
The Song is You
Things To Come
Tippin'
Transitions
Trinkle Tinkle
26-2
Webb City
Witch Hunt
Woody n' You
Work
You Say You Care
Yes or No

RHYTHM CHANGES CHORDS

For Rhythm Changes Study on Page 106

‖ B♭Δ7 G7 | C-7   F7 | D-7   G7 | C-7   F7 |

| F-7   B♭7 | E♭Δ7 E♭-7 | D-7   G7 | C-7   F7 ‖

‖ B♭Δ7 G7 | C-7   F7 | D-7   G7 | C-7   F7 |

| F-7   B♭7 | E♭Δ7 E♭-7 | D-7   G7 | C-7   F7 ‖

‖ D7 | D7 | G7 | G7 |

| C7 | C7 | F7 | F7   ‖

‖ B♭Δ7 G7 | C-7   F7 | D-7   G7 | C-7   F7 |

| F-7   B♭7 | E♭Δ7 E♭-7 | D-7   G7 | C-7   F7 ‖

CHECK IT OUT

A Selective Discography of Essential Listening

John Abercrombie - Gateway
John Abercrombie - Timeless

Cannonball Adderley - Live in San Francisco
Cannonball Adderley - Live at the Lighthouse
Cannonball Adderley - Somethin' Else

George Benson - Body Talk
George Benson - Beyond the Blue Horizon
George Benson - Breezin'

Art Blakey - Free For All
Art Blakey - The Big Beat
Art Blakey - Moanin'
Art Blakey - Caravan
Art Blakey - A Night at Birdland

Clifford Brown - Brown/Roach Inc.
Clifford Brown - Live at Basin Street
Clifford Brown - A Study in Brown
Clifford Brown - With Strings
Clifford Brown - Live at the Bee Hive

Ornette Coleman - The Shape of Jazz to Come
Ornette Coleman - Science Fiction
Ornette Coleman - Ornette

John Coltrane - Soultrane
John Coltrane - Blue Train
John Coltrane - Giant Steps
John Coltrane - Coltrane's Sound
John Coltrane - Transition
John Coltrane - Impressions
John Coltrane - A Love Supreme
John Coltrane - Live at the Village Vanguard
John Coltrane - Live at Birdland

Chick Corea - Now He Sings, Now He Sobs
Chick Corea - Inner Space

Miles Davis - Kind of Blue
Miles Davis - Relaxin'
Miles Davis - Milestones
Miles Davis - Live at the Plugged Nickel
Miles Davis - Nefertiti
Miles Davis - ESP
Miles Davis - Miles Smiles
Miles Davis - In a Silent Way

Eric Dolphy - Out to Lunch
Eric Dolphy - Live at the Five Spot

Bill Evans - Live at the Village Vanguard
Bill Evans - Explorations
Bill Evans - Interplay

Dizzy Gillespie - Sonny Rollins/Sonny Stitt Sessions
Dizzy Gillespie - Complete RCA Victor Recordings

Dexter Gordon - Doin' Allright
Dexter Gordon - Go
Dexter Gordon - Generations

Herbie Hancock - Speak Like A Child
Herbie Hancock - Maiden Voyage
Herbie Hancock - The Prisoner
Herbie Hancock - Empyrean Isles

Joe Henderson - Inner Urge
Joe Henderson - Mode for Joe
Joe Henderson - In Japan
Joe Henderson - In n' Out
Joe Henderson - So Near, So Far (w/ J. Scofield)

Freddie Hubbard - Hub-Tones
Freddie Hubbard - Ready for Freddie
Freddie Hubbard - Red Clay
Freddie Hubbard - Night of the Cookers

Andrew Hill - Point of Departure
Andrew Hill - Black Fire

Elvin Jones - Live at the Lighthouse

Booker Little - Out Front

Jackie McLean - Destination Out
Jackie McLean - Capuchin Swing
Jackie McLean - One Step Beyond

Hank Mobley - Soul Station
Hank Mobley - Roll Call
Hank Mobley - Workout

Thelonious Monk - Monk and Trane
Thelonious Monk - Monk and Sonny Rollins
Thelonious Monk - Genius of Modern Music
Thelonious Monk - Criss Cross
Thelonious Monk - Live at the 5 Spot
Thelonious Monk - Monk's Music

Wes Montgomery - Full House
Wes Montgomery - Smokin at the Half Note
Wes Montgomery - Incredible Jazz Guitar
Wes Montgomery - Trio
Wes Montgomery -Impressions

Lee Morgan - Live at the Lighthouse
Lee Morgan - Cornbread
Lee Morgan - Search for the New Land
Lee Morgan - The Sidewinder

Gerry Mulligan - What Is There To Say?

Phineas Newborn - A World of Piano

Charlie Parker - Bird and Diz
Charlie Parker - Jazz at Massey Hall
Charlie Parker - Now's the Time
Charlie Parker - Savoy Sessions
Charlie Parker - Live at St. Nick's

Sonny Rollins - The Bridge (w/ Jim Hall)
Sonny Rollins - A Night at the Village Vanguard
Sonny Rollins - Saxophone Colossus
Sonny Rollins - Tenor Madness
Sonny Rollins - Freedom Suite
Sonny Rollins - Tour de Force

John Scofield - Bar Talk
John Scofield - Blue Matter

Woody Shaw - Love Dance
Woody Shaw - Rosewood
Woody Shaw - Moontrane

Wayne Shorter - Speak No Evil
Wayne Shorter - The All Seeing Eye
Wayne Shorter - Schizophrenia
Wayne Shorter - Adam's Apple
Wayne Shorter - Soothsayer
Wayne Shorter - Ju-Ju
Wayne Shorter - Night Dreamer

Horace Silver - Song for My Father
Horace Silver - Cape Verdean Blues
Horace Silver - Blowin' the Blues Away
Horace Silver - Horace - Scope
Horace Silver - Silver's Serenade

McCoy Tyner - The Real McCoy
McCoy Tyner - Inception
McCoy Tyner - Reaching Fourth
McCoy Tyner - Time For Tyner

Larry Young - Unity